Jeannean Kintner

東
魚

БИБЛИЯ

לא תִרְצָח:

EPAONAPISTOKLEOS

Προκλῆς

ſt modus in rebus: ſunt certi deniqȝ fines

XXXVIII

TYPEWRITER

ABCDEFGHIJKLMNOPQRSTUVWXYZ

Book

1234567890

ABCDefghijklmnopqrstuv

The authors' thanks to Dr. S. I. Hayakawa of the University of Chicago and to Dr. Wilfred Funk for their helpful suggestions regarding the manuscript of this book.

19 20

Printed in the United States of America
by The Garrison Corp.

Library of Congress Catalog Card Number: 54:5947

SBN 531-00673-5

THE First Book OF WORDS

Their Family Histories

By Sam and Beryl Epstein

Pictures by Lászlo Roth

FRANKLIN WATTS
NEW YORK

The story of a word

Hello!

Do you know what that word means? Of course you know what you mean when you say it. But did you know that just a hundred years ago there was no word hello? In those days people said "How do you do?" or "Good morning," whenever they spoke to each other, and they could speak to each other only when they saw each other.

Then Alexander Graham Bell invented the telephone, and people could talk to each other even when they were far apart. Everybody thought the new invention was wonderful. When a person heard a voice speaking over the telephone from miles away, he was too excited to say, "How do you do?" or "Good morning." But he was also afraid the person at the other end of the wire wouldn't hear him unless he shouted. So he called

out "Hollo!" This was a very old word that farmers and hunters used to call to someone far away.

After a while, people changed the word a little and called "Hello!" instead. Pretty soon they knew they didn't have to shout at all. But by that time the word had become a habit, and today Americans still say "Hello" when they pick up the telephone.

This example shows how new words are born whenever they are needed. New words are being invented all the time. Perhaps you invented a new word today yourself to describe a new way you felt or a new thing you made.

Some new words become a part of a language, just as hello did. That word was kept because it is so useful. Other new words that are not so useful may be forgotten quickly. The world is changing all the time, and so words change too, to keep up with it.

Every word is a puzzle

Every word has a kind of secret story behind it, just as hello has. Each word is a puzzle, and it's fun to find the answers.

Some of the puzzles are easy to solve. The word **breakfast,** for example, is made up of two smaller words, break and fast. You know what break means. And when someone is said to fast, it means he doesn't eat. Most people fast from the time they go to bed until they get up in the morning. They break their fast when they eat breakfast.

But some word puzzles are a little harder. The word **paper** comes from the name of a plant called papyrus. Papyrus grows in hot climates, especially in Egypt, along the Nile River. In ancient times in the land of Egypt men learned how to mash

the papyrus plant into a pulp, flatten it out and let it dry into a thin sheet. They used the sheet to write on. That's why today the word paper, from papyrus, is used for sheets that are written on – even though today's paper is not made of papyrus at all.

Umbrella comes from the Latin word *umbra,* which means shade. The Italians took that word to make the word umbrella, which means "a little shade." In their hot sunny land they needed an umbrella to give them a little shade from the sun. The English word was borrowed from the Italians, but its meaning changed. You don't use an umbrella when the sun is shining. Instead you use it when it rains.

This is a good example of how words sometimes stay the same even when their meaning changes.

Words are important

Did you ever wonder how people would get along if they had no words?

Without words they couldn't talk to each other. They couldn't ask questions or give answers. They couldn't learn anything except by finding it out for themselves. Nobody could tell anyone else that fire is hot. A person could learn that only by burning himself.

Without words there would be no newspapers to report what is going on in the world, and no books full of stories and facts. You couldn't make a cake or a model airplane, because you couldn't ask anybody how to do those things or read words that would tell how to do them. No one could learn to be a doctor or a nurse or an engineer no matter how much he wanted to do so because nobody could tell or write down in a book all the things a doctor or a nurse or an engineer needs to know.

In fact, if there were no words, there wouldn't *be* any doctors or nurses or engineers – or airplane pilots or storekeepers or teachers or anything else you can think of – because words are necessary tools for almost every kind of work that is done in the world.

What is a word?

Did you ever stop to think what a word is?

It is just a sound or a group of sounds that means something in a particular language.

Of course people can make sounds that don't mean anything. They can make the sound GUNG, for example. But if your friend asks you if you want some candy and you say, "Gung," he doesn't know whether you want the candy or not. The sound you made didn't have any meaning in English. If you really want the candy you will make sounds that have meaning in your language. You will say, "Yes, please," or "Thanks, I'd love to have some candy."

Written or printed words are not sounds, but they are symbols, or signs, for sounds. Written words have a much shorter history than spoken words, and printed words have the shortest history of all.

People spoke words long before they wrote them down and very long before they learned how to print them with machines. The spoken word is probably almost as old as man himself.

There are different kinds of words in different parts of the world. In France and China and Mexico and Russia and in many other places people don't speak the same words you do. They use different words and put them together differently. Sounds that have meaning for them may have no meaning for you. (If somebody says *gung* in China, for example, his friend will know what he means. *Gung* is a Chinese word that means common.)

English is a popular language

All over the United States, and in Great Britain, Canada, Australia and New Zealand, most people speak English most of the time. People in other lands also learn to speak English sometimes in addition to their own language.

Today English is one of the most popular languages in the world. Half the world's newspapers are printed in English, and three-quarters of the world's broadcasts are spoken in English.

But there was a time when not very many people spoke English. Does that surprise you? And does it surprise you to know that a language has a history, just as a country has a history?

The history of the English language is just as exciting as the history of the United States. It is a story of long voyages and wars, of discoveries and inventions. It begins in Europe, from which many Americans originally came. And it is still going on today, just as the history of this country is going on. No one knows what the United States will be like a hundred years from now because it is still changing every day. No one knows what the English language will be like a hundred years from now either, because it too is changing every day.

Families of languages

In the nineteenth century scholars worked out a fascinating kind of "family history" of the great group of languages to which English and most European languages belong. They noticed that these languages had similar root words and similar ways of expressing the same ideas. Take the word "father," for instance. In German it is *vater;* in Latin, *pater;* in Greek, *pater;* in Sanskrit, *pitar*.

At one time long, long ago, they reasoned, there may have been one language from which all these languages grew, just as a family begins with one set of parents. They called the languages that seemed to belong to this family the Indo-European (IN-doh YOOR-uh-PEE-un) group. The scholars thought the original language must have had words for all the things that are important

to all people — words like mother and father, food and water.

There weren't many people who spoke that original language because thousands of years ago the world's population was much smaller than it is now. But those people were nomads, or wanderers. They didn't have farms or build cities. The only way they got food was by finding wild fruits and nuts and by catching fish and wild animals. And as they wandered in search of food they became scattered over parts of Europe and Asia.

After a while these people stopped being nomads. They learned how to plant crops and became farmers. Little groups settled down here and there and began to build real homes and live in villages and towns. Soon the language of each group was changing and gaining new words so that the people could talk about their new way of life. After a while each group had its own language. It was still a little bit like its "brother" languages, but it was growing more different every year. Finally the various languages were so different that the people in one place couldn't understand the people who lived in another place some distance away.

You can imagine what happened if you think of a father with, say, four sons named John and James and Charles and Joseph. As each son grew up and decided to settle in his own house, the father gave him a table just like the table he himself had always used. But each son found he needed more than just a table in his new home, and so he made chairs and beds and all the other

things he wanted. He even changed his table a little bit to suit himself. John and James lived near each other and liked the same things. They helped each other, and when their homes were finished they looked quite a lot alike. The same thing happened with Charles and Joseph. Their two houses looked quite a lot alike too. But even so, when the father visited his sons after a while, he was very surprised to see the four kinds of homes that all had been built around one kind of table.

In the same way, scholars believe, many different kinds of languages were built around the words of one parent-language.

This chart shows some of the groups of Indo-European languages and their modern descendants.

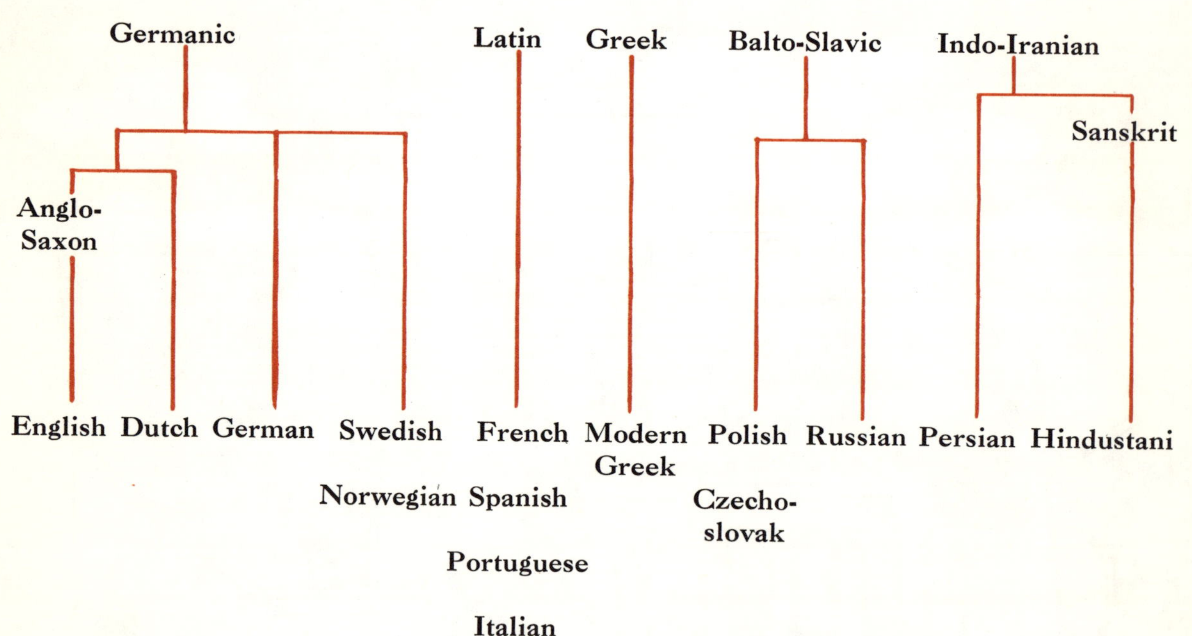

The beginnings of English

Long ago English was spoken only in the country now called England. England itself took its name from a tribe of people known as the Angles, who went to England about 1,500 years ago from their early home in what is now Germany. The Angles, and another tribe called the Saxons, who also moved to England from Germany, took their language with them into their new home. It is sometimes called the Anglo-Saxon (ANG-loh SAK-sun) language. But usually it is called Old English, and this is a good name to use because it is a reminder that this language was the beginning of the English language that is spoken today.

Many things happened to Old English to make it change and grow into the English you speak. But a lot of the words used every day are really Old English words, even though they no longer sound just the way they sounded when the Angles and the Saxons first brought them into England.

The Anglo-Saxons were hunters and farmers, and so of course they had words for all sorts of animals. The modern English words **horse, cow, ox** and **dog** come from their words *hors, cu, oxa* and *docga.* The word **fish** comes from the Old English word *fisc.*

Run, play, work, sing and **eat** come from the Old English words *rinnan, plegan, worc, singan* and *etan.*

Food and **sleep** are from the Old English words *foda* and *slaepan.* **Barn** and **house** and **home,** in Old English, were *bern* and *hus* and *ham.*

Today, when a baby is learning to talk, the first words he learns are usually words that have come down from Old English.

When he points to the different parts of his face and names them all, he is using the modern forms of the Old English words for **eye, nose, mouth** and **chin.** The words **head, neck, arm, hand, finger, leg** and **foot** also come from Old English words.

Red, green, blue, yellow, brown, black – the names of all those colors come from Old English. So do the numbers from one to a hundred.

Of course if someone who lived in the days of the Anglo-Saxons could suddenly visit this country today, he probably couldn't understand American speech and Americans probably couldn't understand him. The words we use, and the words he would use, would often be almost the same. But he would say them one way and we would say them another. The way people pronounce their words often changes.

Not very long ago, for example, most people said the word "wound," meaning an injury, to rhyme with "sound." Now wound rhymes with "spooned." If the pronunciation of a word can change that much in recent years, you can imagine how much words have changed in the many hundreds of years that have gone by since the time of the Angles and Saxons.

Not long after the Angles and Saxons settled in England, Danes began to raid the country. After a while they settled there too and became friendly with their neighbors. They added many words to Old English. The modern words **take** and **law, sky, skin, skull** – in fact, almost all words beginning with SK – come from the Danes. But Old English did not change much until a very different kind of people came to live in England.

The Norman conquest

In the year 1066 a group of people called Normans, who lived in France, sailed across the narrow channel that separates England from France and conquered England. This was one of the most important events that ever took place in England and it had a great effect on the English language.

For many years after that the kings of England were really French kings. They spoke French, and all the lords and ladies at their court spoke French too. Their palaces were very beautiful. And the French rulers lived in a style that was quite different from the way the earlier English settlers lived.

The English people spent most of their time plowing and harvesting their fields, herding their flocks and weaving the coarse cloth they wore. Of course they had words for all the kinds of work they did. The words **plow, harvest, shepherd, weaver** and **cloth** all come down from Old English. But the French rulers had brought with them people who did other, more elegant kinds of work – carpenters to make their fine houses and fine furniture, painters to decorate them, and tailors to make their fine clothes.

The English people didn't like having French rulers, but they couldn't help admiring the fine way the French people lived. Soon many English people were using some of the strange French words they had heard at the court – words like *fourniture, peintre* and *tailleor*. But they didn't say them in just the same way the French people did. They made the French words their own, and said them in a way that was easy for them to pronounce: **furniture, painter** and **tailor.**

An English farmer still called the woolly animal he tended by its old name, **sheep.** But he learned that when a French nobleman served a sheep for dinner, the nobleman called it by its French name, *mouton*. Englishmen began to call their sheep by the French name when the animals had been killed and the meat cooked. To this day that meat is still called **mutton,** the name that came down from the French.

Other words that are used today for live animals and for cooked meat came down in the same way. The word **pig** comes from Old English, but the word **pork** comes from the French. **Cow** comes from Old English, but no one says he is having cow for dinner. Instead he says, "We are having **beef,**" which comes from the French.

You can see that the French language was quite different from the English language. English, like German, Dutch and Swedish, is called a "Germanic language" because people who study languages believe all these are descended from a common Germanic ancestor. They form one group on the chart on page 12.

This is how the Germans, the Dutch and the Swedes say "Good morning, Father!"

German: Guten Morgen, Vater!

Dutch: Goeden morgan, vader!

Swedish: God morgon, fader!

But French is not very much like any of those languages. Instead it is like other languages spoken in Europe – Spanish, Italian, Romanian and Portuguese – called "Romance languages." All those languages were descended from a common ancestor too. Their ancestor was Latin, the language spoken in ancient Rome. Even today they all have words that are very much alike. This is how the people in those lands say, "Good night, Mother!"

French: Bonne nuit, ma mère!

Italian: Buona notte, madre!

Spanish: Buenas noches, madre!

Portuguese: Boa noite, mãe!

Scholars are quite sure about the way in which Latin developed into several different languages. The story of that development begins when the ancient Latin-speaking city of Rome conquered the rest of Italy and many other parts of Europe and made them all colonies of Rome. The city sent Roman governors and soldiers into all her new colonies to rule the people who lived there. Of course these Romans usually returned home when their period of service was over. But when the Roman Empire broke up about 1,500 years ago, many of the Romans who were in the colonies at that time stayed where they were. They married and raised families there, and their Latin language was adopted by the people they lived with. In each colony, however, the language changed and became a little bit like the language spoken there before the Romans came. In France, for example, Latin gradually changed into the language called French. In the same way, in other places, it changed into the languages called Italian, Spanish, Portuguese and Romanian.

So you can see that most of the French words the Normans brought with them to England were forms of still older Latin words changed to make them easier for French people to say.

The Latin word *libertas,* for example, which means freedom, became the French word *liberté*. Then, when French people took that word into England with them, the English began to use it too. But they didn't say it quite the same way the French did, and that's how the word **liberty** got into English.

Latin and Greek words

A great many Latin words came almost straight into English without going through the French language first. Latin has always been the official language of the Church. All the important ceremonies of an Englishman's life were held in Latin. Scholars used Latin all the time in writing to their friends in other lands. Almost all books were written in Latin, and court trials were held in Latin too. English people began to use Latin words in their own language, pronouncing them, of course, in the way that was easiest and most comfortable for them.

A lot of the words we use today, especially when we are talking about laws and government or religion, come down direct from Latin. For example, the Latin word for laws is *leges*. From that word comes the English word **legal,** which means "according to the law," and **legislator,** which means "one who brings the law," and **legislate,** which means "to make laws." More than half the words in the English language today can be traced back to Latin, directly or indirectly.

Greece was once the center of learning for the whole world. About twenty-five hundred years ago she had the world's best government and the finest artists and greatest writers. But Greece, weakened by many wars, finally was conquered by Rome. The Romans admired Greek art and writing, and borrowed Greek words to use in their own language. Some of these words have come into English by a very roundabout road.

The word **govern,** for example, was once a Greek word, *kybernan,* which means "to steer or rule." When the Romans began to use that word they changed it to make it easier for them to say. It became *gubernare* in Latin. Then the French used the word and it became *gouverner.* And finally the French people brought the word into England, where it became govern.

But Greek words have come into English by another road too, one which is not quite so roundabout. It started about 500 years ago when the Turks conquered the great city of Constantinople. Many Greek scholars were living in that city at the time, and they fled to Rome. There they told Italian scholars and scholars from many other lands about the wonderful books and works of art of ancient Greece. These men had known almost nothing about ancient Greece, and they were very interested. English scholars, like those in Europe, began to use many Greek words, changing them to fit their own language.

English people liked to say those Greek words just as they had liked to say French words. They thought it made them sound as wise as the wisest scholar. A man felt very proud if he could say, "I am a philosopher." The word **philosopher** comes from the Greek *philos,* which means "loving," and *sophos,* which means "wise." A philosopher is someone who loves wisdom.

Do you see why English is called a melting pot? It has all sorts of words in it – Old English or Anglo-Saxon words, Latin words, French words, Greek words and words from many other languages too.

Scholars call the period between 1066, when the Normans conquered England, and 1500, when the greatest number of Latin and Greek words had become a part of the English language, the "Middle English" period. (Geoffrey Chaucer, the famous author of the *Canterbury Tales,* wrote during the fifteenth century.) After that time, even though the English language continued to change, it changed more slowly. "Modern English" is the name scholars have given to the English language from 1500 to today.

How men first wrote their words

The invention of writing happened very slowly, and it took place so long ago that no one really knows much about it. But you can guess why it happened.

People could speak their thoughts. They knew how to put their thoughts into the sounds we call words. But they didn't know how to keep them.

You know that if you tell somebody something, he may forget it. But if you put your thought into written words and give it to him, he can look at the words again whenever he wants to. And whenever he looks at them he will know what you told him. When your words are written down they can't be forgotten.

All writing is just a way of keeping thoughts. Newspapers and magazines and books are thoughts written down so that people can read them, whenever they want to, so that they can keep the thoughts forever and even hand them down to their children's children.

The first kind of writing was what is called picture-writing. Today in America if we want to write about a dog, we write DOG. But people who did picture-writing made a picture of a dog instead, like this:

After a time, people found that they couldn't always make a picture that looked like the thing that was in their minds. They could make a picture that looked like a dog, but they couldn't make a picture that looked like "good" or "comfort" or "true." If they wanted to put down thoughts like that they had to think of special pictures that would express those ideas. When people make pictures like that, they are said to be writing **ideographs.** Graph is from an ancient Greek word that means "writing." You can see that ideograph means "idea-writing."

The Chinese still use ideographs when they write today. Some of the ideographs are so simple that they are almost picture-writing. When the Chinese want to talk about a tree, for example, they say the word *mu,* which means tree or wood in Chinese. But when they want to write that word they don't write the letters M and U. Instead they draw a little picture of a tree, like this: 木 And if they want to write about trees, they don't add a letter S to their word, as English-speaking people do. They make a picture of two trees, like this: 木 木

That picture means more-than-one-tree, or forest.

Here is part of a story written in picture-writing by an American Indian:

It means, "My friend and I went in a canoe to an island to hunt with our bows and arrows. We killed a sea lion."

Picture-writing or ideographs are sometimes used today in this country. Instead of writing the words THIS WAY, you may draw this: ⋙——> Everybody understands what it means. That sign is an ideogram.

If a sign along a road looks like this, you know it means CURVE AHEAD:

Sometimes on a funny valentine you find this:

Probably when people first used picture-writing each man made whatever kind of picture he wanted to make. If he wanted to write about an ox, he might draw this or this or this . But after a while, all the people in one part of the world agreed that certain pictures would mean certain things. Then they could understand each other's writing.

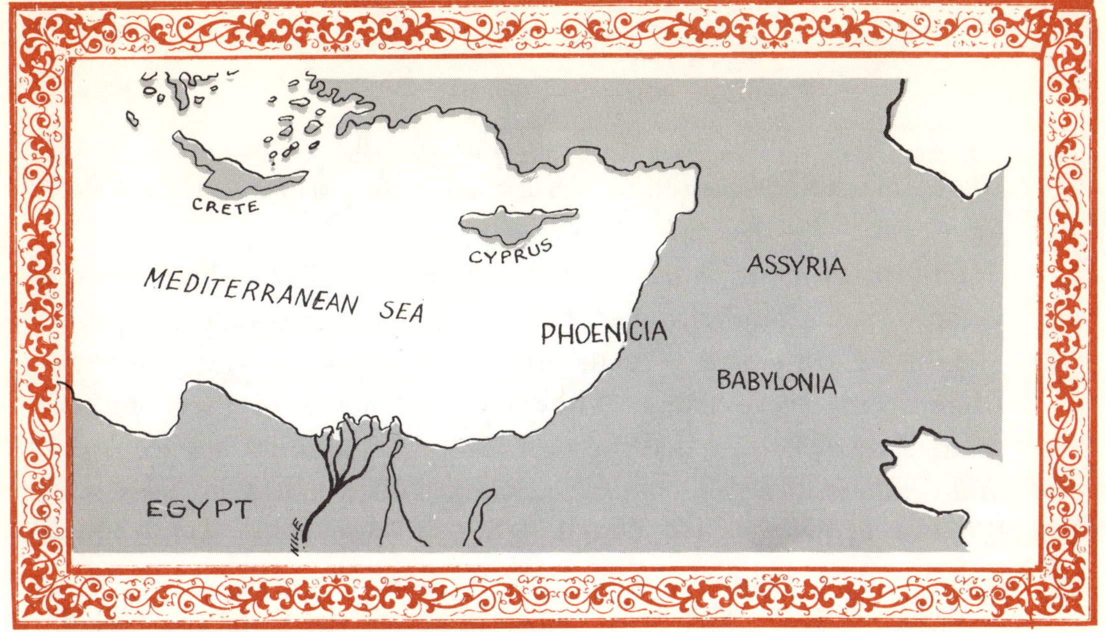

The alphabet is born

In the ancient land of Phoenicia (fuh-NISH-uh), about three thousand years ago, people who wanted to write down the idea of an ox made this little picture which looked to them like the horns of an ox. If they wanted to write "door," they made this picture . Their word for ox was *aleph*. Their word for door was *daleth*.

The Phoenicians had to learn a new picture for every single word. It took a long time for a man to learn the pictures for all the words he might want to write. And so, after a while, the Phoenicians began to work out a new method of writing. Instead of using the picture to mean *aleph,* or ox, they used that picture for the first sound in the word *aleph* – the sound of A. Instead of using to mean door, or *daleth,* they used it for the first sound in the word *daleth,* the sound of D. If the Phoenicians had wanted to write the English word AD they would have written it like this: ∀ ∆

The Phoenicians were the only people in the world ever to develop a true alphabet – a system of signs to represent sounds.

After a time the Greeks borrowed most of the signs the Phoenicians were using. They changed some of them to suit themselves. They turned the sign for A upside down, for example, and made it like this: A They also added a few new signs of their own, because the Greek language had some sounds in it that the Phoenician language didn't have.

Then the Romans began to use many of the signs the Greeks were using, and they changed them too. Finally the signs the Romans used plus a few others were used for the writing of English words. The old Phoenician sign for ox had become the letter A, and the old sign for a door had become the letter D. The other letters of the Roman alphabet come down in the same way from those long-ago signs first used in picture-writing.

The English word **alphabet** comes from the two Greek words *alpha* and *beta,* the Greek names for the first two letters in their alphabet. Sometimes English-speaking people call the alphabet the ABCS.

From spoken words to written words

Of course it was much easier for people to write when they had an alphabet. But they still had to decide what letters would best give the idea of the sound of each word.

You know that no two people speak in exactly the same way. You have probably heard the words "Yes, sir," for example, said in many different ways. Some people say "Yes, siR," with a very loud R-sound at the end. Others say, "Yes, suh," as if there were no R-sound at the end at all. And some people say the two words very fast, as if they were just one word, like "Yessir" or "Yassuh."

It isn't surprising, then, that in the early days of English writing people didn't always agree about what letters would stand for the sounds of a certain word. People in different parts of England spoke a little differently. A man who wrote a D and an O and a G for the word DOG might not understand that another man meant to write that same word when he wrote the letters DAWG. Each man wrote a word the way it sounded to him, but it might be confusing for someone else to read if the other person didn't speak just the way the writer did.

From written words to printed words

Even if it was confusing when Englishmen wrote their words in different ways, it was not very important at first. This was because for a long time only a few people – merchants, for example – tried to write words or read the words other people had written. Most ordinary folk got along without ever writing or reading at all.

The only books people had in those days were written out, word by word, by hand. Of course it took a very long time to write each book that way, and hand-written books were rare and costly.

Then, about five hundred years ago, people learned how to print letters with a printing press. A press could print a page

of a book in just a minute. The printing press was a wonderful invention. It made it possible for the world to have a great many books.

Just as soon as there were a lot of books in the world, most people wanted to learn to read. They wanted to become "literate." This word comes from the old Latin word *litera,* which means "letter." A person who is literate knows his letters – that is, he can make words with letters and he can read those words.

In England people began to spell their words the way the printers in London wrote them at that time. London was the capital of England, and the center of its culture. The printers, of course, were writing words in a way that fitted the sound of the words as they said them.

Now you can understand why the spelling of some words seems strange today. It is because most English-speaking people no longer say these words as people said them at one time, even though the words are still spelled in the same way.

If a present-day American were going to decide, right this minute, how to spell the word RIGHT, for example, he would probably decide to write it like this: RITE, because those letters show the way it is pronounced. The word THOUGHT might be spelled like this: THOT.

But when people spelled those words at the time the printing press was perfected, they chose a spelling that fitted the way they said the words. In London, about five hundred years ago, people pronounced both those words with a sort of cough in the middle, something like this: RIHKT or RI-GH-T and THOHKT or THO-UGH-T.

Perhaps someday English-speaking people will change the system of spelling so that it fits the way English words sound today. Spelling words in a certain way is really just a habit. And habits can be changed.

English comes to the New World

After Columbus discovered America, and English people began to settle in the New World, they brought their language with them. By then many people could read and write, and they had agreed on the spelling of most words. They spoke and wrote Modern English words in very much the same way they are spoken and written today.

Many new things have happened to the English language, though, since those settlers brought it to America. First it borrowed some Indian words – words that the white settlers heard the Indians say, and which they began to use themselves because they found them very useful. Sometimes they began to use an Indian word because it was a name for a new thing which the white people had never seen before.

When they saw Indian corn, for example, they didn't know what to call it because they had never seen corn in England. The Indians said they called it *maize,* and so the white people began to call it **maize** too. The white people had never before seen corn and beans cooked together either, and so they called

that dish by its Indian name, **succotash.** *Askutusquash* was the Indian word for another vegetable the white settlers had never seen before, but they thought that word was too long, so they shortened it to **squash.**

The Indians wore a special kind of soft shoe which they called a **moccasin** (MOK-a-sin), and that is its English name today. Of course the Indians had their own names for many rivers and mountains, and the settlers began to use those words too. **Mississippi** is an Indian word that probably meant great river.

English-speaking Americans also have borrowed words from other settlers too, from people who came to the New World from Holland, France, Spain and other countries.

The Dutch word koolsla (KOOL-slah), for example, which means "cabbage salad," became **coleslaw.** Americans also borrowed the words **cruller** and **cooky** and **waffle** and **Santa Claus** and **boss** and **sleigh** from the Dutch.

From French explorers and settlers came the word **prairie,** which means "big meadow." The French word *chaudière* (shoh-dee-AIR), which means "a big pot," became the English word **chowder.** Even today, when a cook makes a corn chowder or a clam chowder, she usually makes a big pot of it. And the word **gopher** probably comes from the French word *gaufre* (GOH-fr) which means "honeycomb." The French settlers probably noticed the honeycomb of tunnels which a certain little prairie animal makes underground, and gave him a name that described the tunnels that were part of his home.

From the Spanish settlers English has borrowed the word *cucaracha* (koo-kuh-RAH-chah) and changed it into **cockroach.** And Americans changed the Spanish word *calabozo* (kah-luh-BOH-thoh), which means "jail," into **calaboose.** When the word **key** is used to mean a low island, or reef – as in the name of Key West, for example – it is really a form of an old Spanish word, *cayo* (KAH-yoh).

Words borrowed from all over the world

The English language is rich in words borrowed from all over the world. Travelers to distant lands bring new words home with them. Soldiers who go overseas to fight come back with new words. And the many different people who come to the United States to live, from many foreign countries, bring with them their own words – and the ones that are useful become part of the language.

Here are some words from far countries:

Candy comes from Sanskrit, an ancient language once spoken in India. The Sanskrit word is *khanda,* which means "piece," but it was often used to mean a piece of sugar. The word candy, of course, means a piece of anything sweet.

Tea comes from a Chinese word that sounds very much like it. China produces a great deal of tea.

Assassin comes originally from Arabic, and has a very strange history. About nine hundred years ago, in a certain land in the East, a group of men formed a secret society. They hated all Christians, and swore to kill Christians secretly, by night. In order to make themselves feel fierce enough to kill, they used a powerful drug called hashish. So they came to be called *hashshashin*. The word has changed over the years to assassin, and it is used now for any person who undertakes to kill someone.

Chimpanzee comes from a West African language. It is the natives' name for a kind of small ape.

Kayak comes from the Eskimo word for the small skin-covered boat they use.

Invented words

On the first page of this book you learned how the word hello was first used over Alexander Graham Bell's new telephone.

But where did the word **telephone** itself come from?

Alexander Graham Bell invented that too. He made his new word out of two Greek words, *tele* and *phone*. *Tele* means "far" and *phone* means "sound." A telephone does just what its name says: it sends sounds a far distance. When people use a telephone they can speak across space.

Many inventions got their names in much the same way. Several use that same Greek word, *tele*.

Tele+graph, from a Greek word that means "write," gives **telegraph.** When you telegraph to someone you are writing across space.

Tele+vision, from a Latin word that means "sight," gives **television.** When you sit in your living room and watch people on a television screen, you are seeing across space.

Auto is from a Greek word that means "self," and it too has been very useful when men had to invent new words.

Auto and mobile, from a Latin word that means "moving," gives **automobile.** When Henry Ford built his first car he was making something that moves by itself.

Micro, from a Greek word that means "small," has also been useful when people had to invent a new word for a new thing.

Micro+scope, from a Greek word that means "to look at," gives **microscope,** the name of an instrument through which you can look at small things. Through a microscope you can see the tiniest germ.

Micro+photograph gives **microphotograph,** the word that is used for a tiny photograph.

Now you see how new words can be invented by taking old words from different languages and putting them together. You can solve more word puzzles for yourself. For example, you can figure out where the word **autograph** comes from. You remember that *auto* means "self" and that *graph* means "write." Yes – an autograph is something a person writes himself. Usually the word is used to mean a person's own name, written by himself. Many people collect the autographs of their friends or of famous people.

Words from the names of famous people

Sometimes, too, somebody's name becomes a word for every-day use.

Sandwich comes from the name of an English nobleman, the Earl of Sandwich. The Earl was a very busy man and he hated to interrupt what he was doing to have a meal. So he invented a new and convenient kind of food. He put two pieces of bread together with meat or cheese between them, and made what is now called a sandwich.

Pasteurize comes from the name of a famous French scientist, Louis Pasteur, who first proved that some diseases were caused by germs. He invented a system of heating milk and quickly cooling it again, in such a way that all the harmful germs in it were killed. Almost all the milk that is drunk in this country today is safe because it has been treated in this way. It is pasteurized.

Spoonerism is a funny word for a funny thing. It comes from the name of the Reverend W. A. Spooner, who often had trouble with words. He was always getting them mixed up. If he wanted to say, "May I show you to another seat?" he got mixed up and said instead, "May I sew you to another sheet?" When a person gets mixed up in the same way he is said to have made a spoonerism.

Watt comes from the name of a Scottish scientist, James Watt. James Watt made the first really good steam engine and discovered a great many new things about power. So today electric power is measured by watts. You say, "This is a 60-watt light bulb" or "This is a 1,000-watt toaster."

Watch for brand names

Brand names are like the brand marks a ranch owner puts on his cattle. A brand mark means, "This is my mark. This cow belongs to me." A brand name means "This is my mark. I made this."

Look through the ads in any newspaper or magazine and you will find lots of brand names. They are all special words invented to describe a special thing somebody makes. Here are some of them:

The name **Frigidaire** tells that the air inside the refrigerator is so cold or frigid that it will keep food safe.

A **Mazda** light bulb gets its name from Ahura Mazda, an ancient Persian god. The god's special sign was a bright flame.

Pyrex gets its name from *pyros,* the Greek word for heat or fire. You can put a Pyrex dish inside a hot oven and it won't break.

An **Eversharp** pencil doesn t have to be sharpened. It is, as its name says, forever sharp.

Stuck-together words

There is still another way in which words come into the English language and this is probably the most common of all. New words come into being all the time when two old words are put together as if they were one word.

Some of the stuck-together words are so old that it's hard to believe that each was once two words instead of one.

Already was once all ready.

Nothing was once no thing.

Midnight was once mid night, or middle of the night.

It's easy to guess that **overalls** are clothes worn over all others.

Driftwood is wood that has drifted ashore.

A **downpour** is rain that pours down – not just a drizzle.

A **floodlight** is a light so big that it floods a whole room or stage.

A **merry-go-round** is a thing that goes gaily around and makes you feel merry when you ride on it.

A **slowpoke** is someone who pokes slowly along.

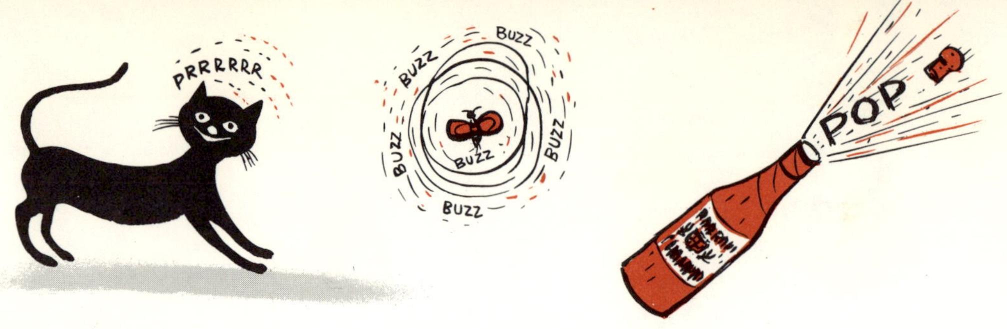

Words that sound like what they mean

Long ago a man listened to a happy cat make the sound "Prrr-r-r-r," and he said, "The cat is **purring.**" The sound of what the cat was doing became a word that meant that special sound.

Other words have come from sounds too.

Listen to the sound a bee makes and you will know why that sound is called a **buzz.**

Listen to the sound of a tight cork coming out of a bottle. "Pop!" is the sound it makes – and **pop** is the English word for it.

Listen to the sound of people whispering together – and you will know where the word **whisper** comes from.

Listen to a small brook running over stones, and you will know why the brook is said to be **murmuring.**

Long ago somebody listened to the sound of bells tinkling and jingling together, and invented a word for the way they sounded. The word was **tintinnabulation** (tin-tin-nab-you-LAY-shun).

People still name a thing from the sound of the thing itself. In fact there is a special word for this kind of name-making. The word is **onomatopeia** (ON-uh-MAHT-uh-PEE-uh) and it comes from the Greek words that mean "names" and "make."

Tricks with words

You have seen a magician do tricks. He shows you a glass of milk, waves a handkerchief over it – and the milk is changed to ink. One minute you see white milk. The next minute you see black ink. One minute you see one thing. The next minute you see its exact opposite.

You can do the same kind of trick with words.

You can take the word **visible,** which means "something that can be seen," add two letters to it and make **invisible** – which means "something that cannot be seen."

Sometimes you may add un- or dis- instead, and do the same trick. Like this:

Food is necessary in order to keep alive.	Chewing gum is unnecessary in order to keep alive.
These children agree.	These children disagree.

Those handy little groups of letters – in-, un- and dis- – are called **prefixes.** The *pre* in that word means "before," or "in

front of." Fix means "fasten." A prefix is something fastened to the front of a word to change its meaning.

There are many other prefixes too. All of them do clever tricks with words.

Take the little word **port,** for example – the English word for a place where ships come and go, carrying goods and people. There is a Latin word, *portus,* that means the same thing. It comes from another Latin word, *portare,* which means "to carry." So whenever you want to talk about carrying something you can usually do it by performing some kind of trick with the little word port and a prefix:

If you add *ex,* which means out of or away	you get **export,** which means to carry out of or away.	England exports machinery to many countries.
If you add *im,* which is a form of in	you get **import,** which means to carry in.	America imports tea from China.
If you add *re,* which means back (or again, as in retake)	you get **report,** which means to carry back.	He will report the news to his school paper.

If you add *trans,* which means across	you get **trans-port,** which means to carry across.	Ships transport goods to Europe.
If you add *sup,* which is a form of *sub,* and means under	you get **support,** which means to carry something by being under it.	These pillars sup-port the roof.

There is another way to perform tricks with words. You do it by adding certain groups of letters at the end of the word instead of at the beginning. These groups of letters are called **suffixes,** because they are "fastened under" or at the ends of words.

Take the word **child,** for example, and add to it the suffix -hood. You get **childhood,** the state of being a child. Add the suffix -ish and you get **childish,** like a child. **Childishness** means childish behavior. **Childless** means without a child, having no children.

Now add some suffixes to port and see what happens.

If you add *-able,* which means capable of	you get **port-able,** which means that a thing can be car-ried.	John has a port-able radio.

If you add *-er,* which means one who	you get **porter,** which means one who carries.	The porter has your trunk.
If you add *-age,* which means the act of	you get **portage,** which is the act of carrying.	Indians portage their canoes from one stream to another.

And if you add suffixes to some of the words made from port on pages 46 and 47, you get words like **transportation** and **important.**

These aren't all the prefixes or all the suffixes, but even these few will show you how easy it is to make words by this clever method – to change the meaning of words as quickly as a magician changes milk into ink, or a cane into a bouquet of flowers.

A new twist for old words

Sometimes when a word is needed for something new, we don't invent a new word. Instead we take an old one and give it a new meaning. The newspapers and everyday talk are full of these new-old words.

When airplane pilots needed a word that meant landing flat on a field, they borrowed an old word that meant something very flat – the word **pancake.**

This is a pancake.

This is a pancake landing.

Once the word **knockout** was used only when people were talking about prize fighters and prize fighting. Now the meaning of that word has grown. It is used to speak of the final winning blow in any sort of contest.

This is a knockout in the ring.

The air force supplied the knockout blow and the enemy surrendered.

Long ago the word **shrimp** meant any small thing. It came from the German word *schrumpfen,* which meant shrivel, and a shrimp was anything that looked shriveled or shrunk. Then people began to use that word for a certain kind of small shellfish that looked shriveled. Today the word is used both ways.

The smallest boy in the class was known as the Shrimp.

I like fried shrimp.

Slang words and how they happen

Sometimes slang words are like the words we have been talking about. They are old words with new meanings.

This isn't slang	*This is slang*
I'm kneading dough for bread.	I have enough dough for an ice-cream soda.
I'll put the smallest block on top.	I'll knock your block off.

But sometimes new slang words are made up. Sometimes they sound funny and sometimes they rhyme. You say, "I don't like rats. They give me the **heebie-jeebies.**"

Or slang words are made by putting two old words together and giving them a brand new meaning. Usually this new word is a quick way of saying something.

Instead of saying, "It is his job to hop up and report to the hotel desk every time the manager rings the bell," you say, "He's a **bellhop.**"

Instead of saying, "He stretches his neck in all directions as if it were made of rubber," you say, "He's a **rubberneck.**"

Sometimes slang words last only for a short time. They become a fad for a few weeks or a few months and then they are forgotten. That's what happened with the word **skiddoo.** About thirty years ago it was a very popular slang word. It meant "Go away. Get out." People used it all the time – and then they forgot about it. After a while, there was a new slang word that meant the same thing. It was **scram.** Perhaps that one will soon be forgotten too.

Sometimes slang words are so useful that they remain. Bellhop and rubberneck are two slang words that were kept because no better or quicker way has been invented to say what those words mean. **Sorehead** and **killjoy** are two more like these.

It would be fun to make a list of today's slang words in a scrapbook. You might put a cross beside each word you think will last for a long time. Then you might put the scrapbook away for a while. When you got it out again you could see if you had put the crosses beside the right words. Perhaps the very words you thought would last would already have been forgotten by that time.

Some words are twins

Some words have more than one meaning. They sound alike, and they are spelled alike, but they can fool you if you don't think fast.

This is a date: July 4, 1776. But a date is also a small brown fruit that is good to eat.

You can strike a match. But you can play a match, too, on the tennis court or the hockey field.

A ball is a round object that is thrown or bounced. But a ball is also a big dance.

The sound a dog makes is a bark. But the outer covering of a tree trunk is also bark.

Sometimes there are two words that sound just alike but are not spelled the same way and don't mean the same thing.

You can break a dish. But you can also step on the brake if your bicycle is going too fast and you want to slow down.

If you go by a store, you go past it. But if you go into the store you can buy something.

There is a bear in his cage at the zoo. And if his fur is all rubbed off in one place, he has a bare spot.

You may wonder why a dog is wagging his tail. And if you like, you can make up a tale about him.

Would you guess they were related?

Sometimes brothers and sisters look very much alike. Sometimes they are so different that it's hard to believe they belong to the same family. Words are the same way. Words that look very unlike and that mean very different things sometimes have the same ancestor and are really related to each other.

Would you guess that **result** and **somersault** have the same ancestor? They do. The second part of both words comes from the Latin word *saltare,* which means "to leap" or "spring." Whatever springs from your work is the result of your work. But if you spring over, you are doing a somersault.

Volume and **revolution** are also related. They both come from the Latin word *volvere,* meaning "to turn." When people start a revolution they are turning against their government. Now a volume is a book with separate pages, but once it was one long page turned around a stick and rolled up like a window shade.

Where does your first name come from?

Most names are very old. Boys have been named John and girls have been named Mary for many hundreds of years.

These names are used in many countries, too – not just in our own. But other people don't always spell them the way we do or pronounce them the way we do.

In France John is **Jean** (ZHON) and Mary is **Marie** (ma-REE).
In Spain John is **Juan** (WON) and Mary is **Maria** (mah-REE-ah).
In Russia John is **Ivan** (EE-von) and Mary is **Marya** (MAHR-yah).
In Italy John is **Giovanni** (gee-uh-VON-nee) and Mary is **Maria** (mah-REE-ah).
In the Netherlands John is **Johann** (YOH-han) and Mary is **Maria** (MAHR-yah).

Jack and **Jock** are other forms of the name John. **Marion** and **Marietta** are other forms of the name Mary.

Some names have special meanings.

Albert and **Alberta** come from a Germanic word that means "nobly bright."

Charles and **Charlotte** come from a Germanic word that means "strong."

Francis and **Frances** come from a Germanic word that means "free."

Louis and **Louise** come from a Germanic word that means "famous warrior."

Paul and **Pauline,** or **Paula,** come from a Latin word that means "small."

Philip and **Philippa** come from a Greek word that means "lover of horses."

Robert and **Roberta** come from a Germanic word that means "bright in flame."

William and **Wilhelmina** come from a Germanic word that means protection.

Margaret means "a pearl."

Peter means "a rock."

Samuel means "asked for of God."

David means "beloved."

Stephen means "a crown."

John means "gift of God."

Thomas means "a twin."

Alice means "truth."

Anne, Nancy and **Hannah** all mean "grace.

Dorothy means "gift of God."

Elizabeth means "consecrated to God."

Susan means "a lily."

Last names came later

Long ago people had only first names. A man was called John or Peter or David. It was the only name he had.

But when many Johns and Peters and Davids all lived in one village, they got mixed up. People had to invent a way to tell them apart, so they would know which John or Peter or David they were talking about.

If a man named John had a father who was also named John, people might call him John, John's son. Or they might shorten it and call him John Johnson, or shorten it even more and call him John Jones. If his brother was named Peter, he might be called Peter Johnson or Peter Jones.

The name Peterson came about in the same way. So did Jackson. So did Wilson, short for Will's son or William's son. So did Anderson, short for Andrew's son, and Davidson or Dawson, short for David's son. Jenkin was a sort of pet name for John, and from it came Jenkinson or just Jenkins. The pet name for Peter yielded Peterkin and Perkins.

Mac or Mc mean "son of," and that's how names like Mac-

Gregor, meaning son of Gregory, and MacDonald, meaning son of Donald, and McTavish, meaning son of David, came about.

There are other ways of saying "son of" too.

Fitz, for example, is a form of the French word *fils* (FEES), which means "son," and so there are names like Fitzpatrick and Fitzgerald, which mean son of Patrick and son of Gerald.

Sometimes people took a name from the place where they lived. A man named John who lived in the village of Hale might come to be known as John Hale. Or if he lived near the village green he might come to be called John Green.

Sometimes people took names from the way they looked. If a man named John was very tall, he might come to be called John Long or John Lang or John Longfellow. If his hair was very light he might be called John White, and if it was dark he might be called John Brown or John Black.

And sometimes people took names from the work they did.

If John had a mill, he might be called John Miller.

If he was skillful with his bow and arrow he might be called John Archer.

If he wove cloth he might be called John Weaver or John Webb or John Webster.

If he baked bread he might be called John Baker, and if he was a good cook he might be known as John Cook.

These second names were so useful that people kept them. They handed them down from father to son until they became what they are today – family names, which belong to a whole family.

Did you know?

That when we talk about a lot of cats we just say "a lot of cats," but that there are special words to use to talk about other animals?

We call a lot of dogs "a pack of dogs."
We call a lot of cows "a herd of cows."
We call a lot of quail "a bevy of quail."
We call a lot of bees "a swarm of bees."
We call a lot of fish "a school of fish."
We call a lot of geese "a gaggle of geese."
We call a lot of lions "a pride of lions."

That demi and semi and hemi all mean half, and that usually we only use one – as in demigod and semifinal and hemisphere – but that there is one word that uses all of them?

In music a **hemidemisemiquaver** is a half of a half of a half of an eighth note, or a sixty-fourth note.

That you can read this sentence backwards and forwards?

I saw Eve was I.

That some people think the phrase **cellar door** is the most beautiful in the English language? They like to say it over and over, as if they were singing a little song:

cellar door . . . cellar door . . . cellar door

What do you think? What word do you like best to say, just for its sound?

That the word **poet** means a maker? Some poets make music with words and some make word-pictures.

Doesn't this make a picture in your mind as clearly as if the poet had used paint instead of words?

> Then I saw the Congo, creeping through the black,
> Cutting through the jungle with a golden track.
>
> —VACHEL LINDSAY

Can you make words paint a picture?

The book of answers

Would you like to know where you can find the answer to many more word puzzles, and the secret story behind most English words?

You can find them in the dictionary.

Some people look in a dictionary only when they want to find the answers to these questions:

How is this word usually spelled?
How do people say this word?
What does this word mean?

The dictionary gives the answers to those questions too. But – unless your dictionary is a very small one – it will also give you the answer to this question:

Where did this word come from and what is the story behind it?

There is a very interesting story, for example, behind the name of the common flower called the **dandelion.** The dictionary tells that story. Look up the word and this is what you will find, right after the dictionary tells you how to pronounce the word:

F. *dent de lion* lion's tooth, fr. L. *dens* tooth *leo* lion.

Perhaps you will think that doesn't look like much of a story,

but you must remember that the dictionary uses a lot of abbreviations. That word, **abbreviation,** comes from the Latin word *brevis,* which means short. An abbreviation is a short way of saying or writing something. In the front of the dictionary you will find an explanation of all the abbreviations it uses. There you will learn that

F. stands for "French"
L. stands for "Latin"
fr. stands for "from."

And now you can read the story behind the word dandelion like this: It comes from the French words *dent de lion,* which mean "lion's tooth." The French words came from the Latin *dens,* meaning "tooth," and *leo,* meaning "lion."

People first called that flower a dandelion because they thought its leaves looked like the sharp teeth of a lion.

Sometimes, of course, your dictionary will not tell you where a word comes from. Instead it may say "deriv. obs.," which is an abbreviation for "derivation obscure," and means that nobody knows where the word comes from.

Yes, there are still word puzzles in English that have never been solved. But people are working at them, and perhaps someday scholars will know how all the words began. Perhaps someday you will find some of the hidden answers yourself. If you do, you will be what is called an **etymologist** (et-ih-MOLL-uh-jist), which means a person who studies the origin of words.

It's easy to guess why there aren't answers to every single word

puzzle. Because words change so quickly, sometimes nobody can remember where a certain word first came from.

Words are changing this very day. You are helping to change them. And they will go on changing, because new words and new meanings for old words will always be needed in order to talk about the changing world.

You are coming to the end of this book. Perhaps by now you are a **philologist.** Do you know what that word means? The first part of the word means "love" and the next part means "word." Both are from the Greek. A philologist is someone who loves words.

Some people like to collect words as other people collect stamps or stones. Some people like to put words together to make music or pictures. Some people like to put words together to tell a story. And everybody likes to say words and to read them – to follow the path of written words into the world of adventure.

Not everybody can have lots of cars or lots of money, but everybody can have lots of words. New words, old words, long words, short words – all the words in the wonderful English language belong to you the moment you learn them, and they can all be yours for always, to use and to change, to have fun with and to love.

The Phoenician word for	The Phoenician sign was	Greeks changed this to	Romans changed this to	
ox was aleph	OR	THEN TO A	A	A
house was beth	OR	THEN TO B	B	B
camel was gimel	OR	THEN TO Γ	C	C
door was daleth	OR Δ	Δ	D	D
window was he		THEN TO E	E	E
hook was vau	OR	THEN LOST	F	F
		THEN TO Γ	G	G
fence was cheth	OR	THEN TO H	H	H
hand was yod		THEN TO I	I	I
				J
palm was kaph	OR	THEN TO K	K	K
rod was lamed	OR	THEN TO Λ	L	L
water was mem	OR	THEN TO M	M	M
fish was nun	OR	THEN TO N	N	N
eye was ayin	O	O	O	O
mouth was pe	OR	THEN TO Π	P	P
knot was koph		THEN LOST	Q	Q
head was resh	OR	THEN TO P	R	R
tooth was shin	W OR	Σ	S	S
mark was tahv	+ OR X	T	T	T
		V THEN TO Y		U
			V	V
				W
support was samekh	OR	THEN TO Ξ	X	X
			Y	Y
weapon was zayin	I OR	I THEN TO Z	Z	Z

Contents

東
魚

EPAONAPISTOKLEOS

לא תִּרְצָח:

БИБЛИЯ

Προκλῆς

modus in rebus: sunt certi denique fines

XXXVIII

TYPEWRITER

ABCDEFGHIJKLMNOPQRSTUVWXYZ

die heiligen Schrift

Book

1234567890

ABCDefghijklmnopqrstuv

ΙΧΘΥΣ

PISCIS

Fish

Fish